LIVING WITH ETERNITY...

ALL YOU NEED AT THE CROSS TO LIVE FOREVER

DR. COLIN D. CRAGO

Ordering Information:

Prime Seven Media
518 Landmann St.
Tomah City, WI 54660

Printed in the United States of America

BY THE SAME AUTHOR:

WALKING ON THE INSIDE
-An exposition on Abiding in Christ

VALUE ADDED CHRISTIANITY
-An overview of Evangelistic Enterprise

THE WAY OF CHRIST
-A discipleship pack of loose-leaf studies
suitable for any denomination

ON BEING SANCTIFIED WITH JESUS
-A manual of loose-leaf studies
for growing Christians

Having known Pastor Dr. Colin Crago for three decades, I've personally observed him implementing the spiritual strategies vividly portrayed in his new book, LIVING WITH ETERNITY.

Written with the wisdom of an academic and seasoned by many years of successful ministry, Dr. Crago and his wife Kim have been an enduring inspiration and a trusted source of counsel. I sincerely hope that readers of this book find the same level of success and inspiration that has marked Dr. Crago's impactful life in ministry.

Dr. Wayne C. Gwilliam D. Min. Th.D.
Author of the Potential of Redeem Mind
Founder Director of Ignite Evangelistic Ministry

TABLE OF CONTENTS

INTRODUCTION.

*I*f we have discovered the wonderful love of God we can readily refer to the multitudinous volumes of literature the Church has produced over the centuries of its existence and find answers to problems or directions we happen to need. ***And my God shall supply all your need according to His riches in glory by Christ Jesus.*** (Phil. 4: 19)

Many of us sit in Church Sunday by Sunday, confident of living in eternity forever. hearing stories about great heroes of the faith and their dramatic accomplishments, not realising The Church in the 3rd world is teaching the 1st world that God is well able to use all of its members to accomplish outstanding eternal things. Realizing we have to start somewhere is our biggest problem. We already know we can' t begin at the top but we can find a well trodden path in the swathes of existing literature others have used to lead them into a much fuller and more satisfying experience of what God already has for us; for His Church and for the benefit of others.

Not getting what we want immediately may be actually trying to help us grow into the place Jesus for-ordained for us all to live in – *doing His heavenly will on earth* (Matt. 6: 10; Lk. 11: 2), sensing our unique value and making a difference in the troubled world around us.

Focusing on what God wants rather than on our obvious inadequacies' can lead us into a richer place as we continue to grow into God's eternal plan of overcoming; and being a significant piece of the answer to the world's needs.

We gained all that God had for us the instant we accepted what God accomplished for us in Jesus at Calvary.

What follows could help work this out now!

CHAPTER I

"...LORD, INCREASE OUR FAITH."

(Luke 17: 5)

These four words were spoken by a group of men who had directly witnessed tremendous evidence of faith in action in the life of those to whom Jesus ministered. Their association with the raw spiritual power of Jesus life had washed over them and enabled them to participate in the miracles happening around them (Eg. Luke10). More than anything it had stirred them to understand something of what was happening in the heavenlies as they hungered for more of the same here on earth...

When faith arises usually repentance precedes it (Acts 2: 36 – 38: 20: 21) and confession follows it. Acknowledging our sin and confessing the reality of our life-giver. Repentance is relief from guilt, shame and sin. It is often defined as doing an about-face.

It implies that I was pursuing one direction in life and I change to pursue another. Scripture declares it like this, *'Repentance from dead works ... faith toward God'* (Heb.6: 1). *"Repentance is not just about thinking again, it is about turning our thinking away from mere logic to having the mind of Christ."*[1] *Faith then is both the crown and the enabler of repentance."*

Here is the secret of *"The way, the truth and the life"* (John 14: 6) that Jesus bequeathed us – *"faith working thru' love."* (Gal. 5: 6). It is not a mountain of information for us to enjoy in our heads, it is the experience of a life to be lived in the power of God's Spirit, exulting Jesus for the benefit of God's creation (Rom. 8:19 – 21)

> **"Now faith is the substance of things hoped for,
> the evidence of things not seen."**
> (Heb. 11: 1)

"Now"	– a present reality. It will cost you the future to live in the past.
"Substance of things hoped for"	– a solid ground of God proven grace continually being verified in future expectation.

"Evidence of things – gathered factual reality readily
not seen" available to the spiritual
senses.

"Without faith it is impossible to please God."
(Heb.11:6)

"Faith makes available what God has provided."[2]
It is essential that we get this straight because our
whole existence, temporal and eternal, depends on
it. Faith is a substance of grace! (Rom 12:3) *"For I
say, through the grace given to me, to everyone who is
among you, not to think of himself more highly than
he ought to think, but to think soberly, as God has
dealt to each one a measure of faith."* Faith is given
by what God says! Peter informs us that it comes *"...
by the righteousness of our God and saviour Jesus
Christ..."* (2 Pet. 1: 1). Certainly not by any form of
pride (1 Cor. 13: 4); tho', as the Passion Translation
says *"...the character of a man is tested by giving
him a measure of fame."* (Prov.27: 21). Bill Johnson
observes: *"The surest way for us to fall short is to
promote ourselves."*[3] Grace is not like the law. Its
favour is dispensed before the obedience and the

ability to perform it. Jesus expects us to see from the heart. It is a largely unused potential in every Christian. The Amplified Bible defines the faith of Heb 11: 1: *"NOW FAITH is the assurance (the confirmation, the title deed) of the things [we] hope for, being the proof of things [we] do not see and the conviction of their reality."*

Faith is something we receive not something we manufacture. It is not just wistful thinking. It is positive but not just positive thinking. It is seeing into the unseen heavenly realm. It is catching hold of what God is saying and has given, even when we don't fully understand. It is supernatural. The illustration of sitting on a chair is often used to demonstrate faith. But it requires no faith to sit on a chair which is obviously designed by aeons of experienced chair makers to support you. If it collapses when you sit on it you will likely sue its maker. Faith goes far beyond mental assent and a lifetime of chair-sitting experience.

> *"This is the victory that overcomes the world, even our faith"* (1 Jn. 5:4)

This victory" may be a supernatural gift but it requires reception and development if is to deliver on its promise.

First it requires willingness to change and a desire to know the heart of the Father. To touch His heart of love provides a heavenly resource that informs us of life's true direction. All wisdom and information needed for our success becomes available as our relationship develops with Him. It's not a repetition of what's happening elsewhere or what has happened in the past. It is a fresh, creative thrust of His life within us. Revealed thru' the freedom granted by Jesus great sacrifice. It is a release of the unlimited knowledge of His heart.

Second: life is not theological rationale, it is practical loving experience. To change and develop requires encounters with Jesus. We must develop an intimacy with Him that attunes us from being a servant, instead, enjoying being His friend. It is a shift in values, readily sponsored by sharing His heart's desire, gladly making value changes. His loving presence becomes our greatest asset. Encounters in the spiritual realm continually expose character transformation. Faith provides eyes for the heart.

Third; functional changes in life become radical. It's not just a matter of filling a role in His Church. It is the flowing of His grace producing love and joy in sharing the accomplishment of His goals with Him. It is not working for His favour it is working from His favour. Here is where He trusts us with more of His loving grace and power as we are being changed to be more like Him.

Fourth: identity is established. To realise the Gospel of Salvation has set us on a path of radical character transformation, where we live out of the loving revelation God has given and stand up confidently in it. Our detractors are overcome and we rejoice in our God given identity. Faith has its anchor in the unseen realm. Faith depends on the movement of God. The movement of God depends upon our movement upon what He has already said. (Rom. 10: 17) It is not the repetition of what's happening elsewhere. It has risk attached to it. Risks in the things we do in Church – in our worship, - in our assessment of the prophetic flow of the Holy Spirit in preaching and witness – risks in ministry diversification and direction, confidence coming directly from the loving history of previous reliance in God.

Faith is a combination of revelation in the inward-man and obedience in the outward man. God is speaking all the time! Psalm 19: 1 – 4a *"The heavens declare the glory of God; And the firmament shows His handiwork: 2 Day unto day utters speech, And night unto night reveals knowledge. 3 There is no speech nor language where their voice is not heard: 4 their line has gone out through all the earth, and their words to the end of the world."* Faith captures this unseen word. But it has to be captured in the heart not the head. When it is implanted and engrafted in our spirit (James 1: 21) it brings forth success in what we say. Faith is in the power of the tongue – but not just nice words or lovely sentiments. When we are speaking reality from deep within, God is able to seize upon it and bring it to pass. When our heart brings to our lips positive life-changing Biblical words, God ensures His success. Jesus expects us to see from the heart.

"Our trust and sensitivity to the Holy Spirit promotes obedience which creates movement and momentum. Faith is active. Our mind needs to become

responsive. *This is precisely what being led by the Spirit means.*[4]

F.F. Bosworth is quoted as saying: *"Faith begins where the will of God is known."*[5]

CHAPTER II

WHEN GOD SPEAKS THINGS HAPPEN!

*C*reation came about by what He said! *"By the Word of The Lord the heavens and the earth were made."* (Psalm 33: 6)

Reconciliation came about by what He said! *"In the beginning was the Word, and the Word was with God, and the Word was God. And the Word was made flesh, and dwelt among us (and we beheld his glory, the glory as of the only begotten of the Father,) full of grace and truth ... 'Behold! The Lamb of God who takes away the sin of the world!'* (John 1: 1,

Success comes about by what He says! There is power in what God says! And because we are created in His image there is power in what we say. *"Death and life are in the power of the tongue, and those who love it will eat its fruit."* (Proverbs 18: 21) If we ignore the positivity in this principle then *"The simple moral fact is that words kill."*(Matt.5:22

Success comes to us when we say what He says! *"Words can injure our egos or inflame our hearts – we can instantly change any emotional experience simply by choosing new words to describe to ourselves what we are feeling. If, however, we fail to master words, and if we allow their selection to be determined strictly by unconscious habit, we may be denigrating our entire experience of life.* The Holy Spirit is constrained to quote the Father as saying in Job 16 verse 5: *"But I would strengthen you with my mouth, And the comfort of my lips..."* The late Dr David Cartledge insisted: *"One of the strongest battles faith people ever fight is to resist the seductive song of natural wisdom and clever unbelief."*[6] Wisdom that produces faith must come from God's revelation not from educational or business systems trying to justify themselves to a cynical audience. *"The man or woman who pulls back when opposed has already set the limit of their achievement."*[7] The biggest opponent of faith is not unbelief - it is fear. There is a spiritual continuum with fear on one end and faith on the other. (Unbelief fits somewhere along the scale, according to a person's own spiritual condition).

Fear, faith and unbelief

The Psalmist says: *"I sought the Lord, and He heard me, And delivered me from all my fears"* (Ps. 34: 4). While it is no trouble for God to deliver us from fear and its associated predicaments, there is a more insidious problem for the Christian – the unresolved conflict that exists between faith and unbelief. The actual fact is that both often exist in any situation or circumstance - at the same time. This is a seeming impossibility. Yet, when Jesus went back and visited His hometown He did not do many miracles (Matt. 13: 58). This didn't mean Jesus faith had diminished; it meant the peoples' attitude was not receptive. Belief and unbelief existed in the same vicinity. Easy to see when each one had a different source and therefore a different representation of life.

In Mark chapter 9 following the Disciples unsuccessful attempts to deliver a mute boy (v.17) Jesus described the people as "a faithless generation"(v.19) ; the same as those in Nazareth. In the process of Jesus delivering the boy, He spoke to the boy's father saying: *"all things are possible to him who believes."*(v.23). The boy's father responded with: *"Lord, I believe; help my unbelief!"(v.24)* - belief and unbelief were active within the same person! There was a belief in Jesus but it was not alone in the boy's father. A problem that seems to live in many 21st century Christians and Churches, not limited by any particular denomination - belief and unbelief in the same person or situation.

As a confirmed intense believer in prayer I am constantly assailed by the frustration of so-called "unanswered prayer," both in myself and all the saints of God. *"Why does Heaven sometimes remain silent when we pray from the earnestness of our hearts?"*

In the early part of the 20th century there seemed to be a plethora of 'healer's' circulating within and without the Church.[E.G. people such as Oral Roberts, T. L. Osborn, John G. Lake, Katherine Kuhlman & many others] When someone was not overtly healed the first reason often given (maybe not by the people mentioned above) was 'the person didn't have enough faith.' When the condemnation of this rationale was realised the next excuse often given was, they were actually healed but it was not yet manifest. Jesus and the Apostles never used such excuses – people were either healed or they weren't. The first "excuse" was obviously true – there was not enough faith. But where was this faith to come from; the person themselves, from the one (or the ones) doing the praying, or from the group or congregation if it were in one of those settings.

The second excuse was more complex. If the healing was now within the person how was it to be brought out? Whatever way it was – by prayer, by formula such as Mark 11: 24, or whatever, why couldn't this have been used in the first place? The responsibility had now shifted from the "prayer(s) to the prayee – very convenient.

Jesus did offer one rationale for lack of deliverance: *"However, this kind does not go out except by prayer and fasting."* (Matt. 17: 21; Mk. 9: 21; Dan. 9: 3) If deliverance is to be attempted it should only happen after qualified people (more than one) have discerned the actual spirit and are prepared to work at its removal. This can be very detrimental if deliverance does not happen and the person is left with the tragic possibility of living with an evil spirit within.

We could be still left with the first diagnosis – God still has to provide the faith from somewhere. Prayer and fasting are still a means of healing that can be used.

Fasting sharpens up the spiritual disciplines within a person and enables them to spiritually function more effectively. Isaiah 58 identifies the plusses and minuses about fasting. Verses 1 – 4 talk about the wrong reasons for fasting. Verses 5 – 7 tells us what a true fast should look like. Verse 7 gives a key: do *"not hide yourself from your own flesh?"* Truly, knowing ourselves and our motives is not only a means of ensuring a real fast but also real faith. When we humbly realise who and what we are in Christ something happens in prayer.*"Beloved, if our heart does not condemn us, we have confidence toward God"* (1 John 3: 21) Condemnation is the devil's biggest tool in thwarting spiritual growth and the apparent production of answered prayer. Failing to master words and allowing their selection to be *"From the same mouth come blessing and cursing."* (James 3: 10)

Verse 32 goes on: *"Whatever we ask we receive from Him,"* We need to continually ask the question: *"Why is my heart condemning me?"* (or, should it be honestly, why should my heart be condemning me) The answer lies in the fact that there is some area in my life that I have not submitted to Jesus and received his forgiveness or there is an unreality in the expression of my spiritual life articulated to other people.

Actually there is a lack of acceptance of who we really are and the fact that God fundamentally loves us the way we are. He saved us the way we were and He will continue to love us the way we are. When we accept His love and enjoy it He will bless us by using us in His great plan.

You remember what you experience!

For many people their experience of life has been very negative. Parents often try to improve the experience of their children's lives by drawing attention to their faults in the hope of improving their prospects for the future. Other family and friends concur. The individual progresses thru' different educational institutions and, advertently or inadvertently, teachers and classmates point out the same foibles. Upon entering the workforce, bosses and associates level the same criticisms. The person becomes convinced, inwardly, that all these people are correct and is left in a malaise of conflicting emotions about why he/she is the way they are and therefore of not much value... Faith continually issues from experiencing forgiveness. not in questioning it so no confidence arises.

Perfect love is the means of advancing up the continuum to effective faith. Accepting what Jesus says about you is far more important than what anyone else says. Forgiving them for their ignorance about your life and motivations is only the start. Finding out your true godly gifting must now become the norm from which you operate.

Confidence comes thru' experiencing revelation!

The scripture is the most readily available source of revelation. But, if you just read it to gain more information you will ultimately dry up spiritually and even become argumentative. When you are reading it with the attitude of experimentally receiving and doing it, real revelation and ultimate faith will be visited upon you. It has been said *"We thrive with revelation knowledge but perish without it."*Eph 1:17 says *"that the God of our Lord Jesus Christ, the Father of glory, may give to you the spirit of wisdom and revelation in the knowledge of Him,"*

Confident faith develops as we continually" *trust in the LORD, and do good ... and feed on His faithfulness"* (Ps.37: 3). We extend this faith *"which has been given to us exceedingly great and precious promises, that through these you may be partakers of the divine nature,"* (2 Peter 1: 4)

"Imitate those who through faith and patience inherit the promises." (Heb. 6: 12)

This imitation is not a matter of doing things we see other impressive saints achieving, it is catching hold of the universal principle of revelational grace and faith and **practising it until reality is expressed**. As a first principle you can always learn from someone spiritually trustworthy with whom you have a confident relationship   In Mark 6 there is the story of the feeding of the 5,000 men (v.44) Most religious meetings usually have more women than men in them (E.G. Matt. 15: 38) and that's not saying anything about children who could have been there also. All in all there could have been a gathering of 10 – 15,000 or more. Jesus instruction to the disciples was: *"You give them something to eat"* (v.37).. They responded with the obvious; *"Shall we go and buy two hundred denarii* [about eight month's wages] *worth of bread and give them something to eat?"*

Jesus immediately turned His attention to what they had – five loaves and two fish (v.38) (plus the anointing of the Holy Spirit.). He commanded the Disciples to sit everyone down in an orderly fashion. Jesus, looked up to heaven, blessed the available food, gave it to the Disciples to distribute to everyone (v.41). *"They all ate and were filled"* (v.42). There were 12 baskets of left-overs (v, 43).

Everyone, including the disciples, centred on the eating.. They missed the real miracle – that which drew on the unseen presence of heaven bringing it about. (Matt. 6: 10; Lk. 11: 2). To just be amazed at what had happened to the boy's lunch missed the point.

Immediately (verse 45) Jesus commanded the Disciples to get into their boat and head for the opposite side of the lake giving Him time to pray (v. 46). How He was to get to the other side of the lake was not their concern.

Observing them from His vantage point on the mountain (v. 46) Jesus saw they were in trouble with the elements (v. 48). How He arrived at the middle of the lake so quickly and in such rough weather is not considered. Walking on still water would have been enough of a miracle let alone doing it in such boisterous conditions making it even more amazing.

When the disciples saw Him they thought He was a ghost. Talking to Him and rejoicing as He joined the boat He called for peace causing the storm to abate (v. 51).

Then, the real problem they had, come to the fore – their hearts were hard (v. 52). They had not learned from the event they had just witnessed as the 5,000 men were fed. Hard hearts saw only what was physically around them. That's why the writer to the Hebrews (3: 8 TPT) says: *"Don't make Him angry by hardening your hearts."* Hearts softened by continually living in the grace of The Spirit see heavenly things. If the Disciples had looked at what brought about what had happened as the 5,000 were fed they would have observed the operation of Father, Son and Holy Spirit in action producing a heavenly revelation infusing what was happening on earth – exactly what the disciples needed as they struggled in the boat. Miracles come from the unseen heavenly realm. That's where they should have looked when they were in trouble in the boat. Living in that heavenly dimension is exactly what Jesus wanted for them and for us. *"Your kingdom come on earth as it is in heaven."* (Matt. 6: 10; Lk. 11: 2). Living in His Presence rather than merely trying to obey His principles = faith in continuous action producing real peace.

When God does something it is too easy to get caught up with the usual human thing – being excited with the details of what just happened. The Bible nowhere says "with the mind man believes." Faith does not require understanding to function, it requires trust. Trust in the heavenly dimension. We seem to think faith is what we need when we get into trouble. WRONG – the faith relationship is what we need consistently all the time. It's not 'faith in faith' it's faith in what Jesus has achieved on the Cross

Faith should be the mirror of our spirit. It should be refracting the nature of heaven constantly. Thru' prayer we should be able to pull the heavenly reality into earthly existence. Faith is active, even to the point of violence (Matt. 11: 12). Notice Romans 10: 17 does not say "faith comes from having heard" it is telling us that faith is in the now – we should be hearing from heaven right now.

Often we are caught in prayer that seemingly requires obvious immediate answers but we are not getting them. With faith, in Hebrews 6: 12 is patience. The original Greek word (makrothumia) is not talking about the absence of strain to achieve promises God has made, rather it is referring to the accompanying attitudes of forbearance, longsuffering and fortitude that give special strength to the patience that must accompany faith. Jesus possessed "all longsuffering." [Ie. patience] (1 Timothy 1: 16). In the urgency of presenting the Gospel spoken of in 2 Timothy 4, (often used in ordaining new ministries,) Paul includes forbearance [patience] (v. 2).

The noted evangelist Smith-Wigglesworth said: *"If you want anything from God you have to pray into heaven. That is where it all is. If you live in the earth realm and expect to receive from God, you will never get anything."* [10]

According to Lk. 8: 15, we only bear fruit with patience, Andrew Murray consistently uses the word "longsuffering" instead of "patience." It all has to do with "inheriting the promises." We have many so called "faith teachers," even Faith Churches and Faith Movements but there doesn't seem to be many "patience teachers, Churches or Movements" accompanying them.

Dr David Yonggi Cho, former pastor of the then world's largest church (ultimately reaching a membership of over 750,000), spread his influence throughout the Christian world when he published his book entitled "The Fourth dimension." An advocacy of patiently believing and receiving what he needed from God. The legacy of this work was reduced to a formula for believing and receiving what you wanted from God (in spite of Dr Cho's evidence of patience). This was not a new theology. It had been religiously declared thru' Spirit-inspired churches from their beginnings.

The late Leo Harris, founder of the Christian Revival Crusade in Australia, commented on Jesus words in Mark 11: 24. *"Therefore I say to you, whatever things you ask when you pray, believe that you receive them, and you will have them."* He drew attention to the strength of the word *"ask"* as being the same word the religious leaders used to demand the crucifixion of Jesus. He continued by strengthening the prayer resolve with the word *"believe"* and ultimately with *"receive."* So, it follows that if we demand something from God believing this is what He wants, we can receive it. Obviously, with the success he had in his own personal ministry he must have succeeded in operating this principle at least some of the time.[11] Unfortunately, many people who have tried to use this formula to receive a miracle have failed. Some have tried so hard to believe and receive they have succeeded in straining every muscle and nerve-ending in their body with no result.

Mark 11: 24 is only a part of the total faith revelation of God in Jesus Christ. The remainder of the inspiration of the apostles and prophets collected together in the books of the Bible all have a place too. Abiding in Christ is a key to getting anything of faith happening. To formularise scripture is to put oneself in the position of organizing the almighty into your will instead of His.

The over-riding principle of the sovereignty of God must be brought to bear first before any of the "formula's" can have any effect. It is God who is going to answer the prayer – not the formula.[12] The consistency of scripture is another oft forgotten principle,

In God's attempt to re-establish the reconstituted Jewish nation following its return from captivity He reveals heavenly help available to the earthly leadership. In Zechariah 3 we see these are Angelic and Prophetic, These beings are still available to the earnest seeker today; the Angel to oversee our spiritual cleanliness plus the Prophet to reinforce God-given goals.

CHAPTER III

THE KEY OF WORSHIP

*I*n our efforts to "bring Heaven down to earth" (Matt. 6: 10; Lk. 11: 2) we have gladly, at times, found we have managed instead to be lifted up into the Heavenly realm ourselves. This is what happens when revival touches us. It is wonderful to overhear people testifying to each other of how they were unexpectedly healed and/or blessed during "real worship services" without special prayer. A far cry from what you might expect from a modern western Church service (liturgical, evangelical or Pentecostal) or indeed even from the Jewish Tabernacle\Temple itself.

All of this indicates a vast lack of realisation of what is concurrently transpiring in the Heavenly realm when real worship is taking place. Hebrews 12 is not an Old Testament expectation or some vague ancient right that might be expected to impinge on us from the past. It is a New Testament anticipation of what we should be experiencing now. Verses 22 – 24 might sound very other-worldly, and it is, because it is heavenly. We often use the term "revival" to try to explain it. Revival should be the normal Christian life not something for special evangelical experiences. It does indicate sometimes how sub-normal we actually are. *"But you have come to Mount Zion and to the city of the living God, the heavenly Jerusalem, to an innumerable company of angels,* **23** *to the general assembly and church of the firstborn who are registered in heaven, to God the Judge of all, to the spirits of just men made perfect,* **24** *to Jesus the Mediator of the new covenant, and to the blood of sprinkling that speaks better things than that of Abel."*

"But you have come ..." NOT you are going to come, but if you are touching revival you have already arrived at the Heavenly Jerusalem where the books of heavenly origin prophesied you should always be.

"Zion" is not the physical place in Israel, nor is it the place generally aspired to when we depart this mortal realm.. It is not some unreachable heavenly sphere. It is within you now thru' the Holy Spirit A place Moses obviously found. It is also referred to as

The City of the Living God. The book of Hebrews tells us that Abraham was always looking for this faith city (11: 10 & 16). The author goes on to let us know that it is still coming (13: 14) and we can realise it any time by offering "*a sacrifice of praise*"(13: 15). It is the place of double peace (from "Salem" = peace).

"*A mountain*" always speaks to us as a place of influence. A site of government (judicial & legislative)[7]. Therefore, the Spirit of God within can perform exceptional things within our own spirits to release true righteousness from our hearts; including times of healing, degrees of righteousness, real spiritual worship plus other-world spiritual intensity.

"*Angels*" are often referred to in the scripture and in other visible places. Without getting involved in their various levels of operation, there are so many of them available to us, obviously more than one each, adding to the dynamic government of the mountain and providing individual help to us.

We are registered in Heaven in the one and only Church of the Firstborn, there is a state of spiritual Church unity already in existence which we would do well to draw on in our efforts to forge visible Church unity here on earth.

A place where God is judging (even us) according to that grace already given in the New Covenant thus overcoming the Old Testament law. This is the place where God is looking at the original books of His purpose and comparing them with actual performance and in His justice, working out how in the Heavenly court, mediation on Jesus blood sorts out the spirits of just men and makes them perfect. It is the heavenly place where the better things spoken of are clear and readily understandable to us.[12]

All this is a long-winded way of saying that if we are consistently conscious of the inward heavenly revival. These "*better things*" could include necessary healing being realised.

In 2 Timothy 1: 9 Paul is encouraging young Timothy (as we should all be encouraged) to fulfil what was planned before time began: *"God, who has saved us and called us with a holy calling, not according to our works, but according to His own purpose and grace which was given to us in Christ Jesus before time began."*

Worship begins at the throne room of God (Rev. 7: 9 - 12.). We can get there by trusting the Holy Spirit to get us there. Jesus tells us in John 4: 23 and 24

"But the hour is coming, and now is, when the true worshipers will worship the Father in spirit and truth; for the Father is seeking such to worship Him. 24 God is Spirit, and those who worship Him must worship in spirit and truth." If we are looking to develop real worship it means our relationship has to be deep-rooted in the Holy Spirit.

Secondly it must be truthful. That is, it cannot have selfish undertones of particular personal effects – we must be worshipping God for His sake not ours,

Thirdly, to get there, particularly in a group setting, it will ultimately require real praise that honestly draws the Holy Spirit into the real worship He desires. Worship is the language of Heaven. It establishes a rapport for both you and God. You can share honestly and He can do whatever He thinks is best for you and the existing situation.

Worship creates the atmosphere that the court of Heaven operates from Revelation 7: 11 & 12 - All the angels stood around the throne and the elders and the four living creatures, and fell on their faces before the throne and worshiped God, :12 saying: *"Amen! Blessing and glory and wisdom, Thanksgiving and* *honour and power and might, Be to our God forever and ever. Amen."*

When we really worship we participate in the governmental processes of heaven that touch and change things on earth. It is not just something that gives us shivers up and down the spine or fulfills a required pattern it is something giving out heavenly authority on earth.

"One of the stubbornly enduring habits of the human race is to insist on domesticating God. We are determined to tame Him. We figure out ways to harness God to our projects. We try to reduce God to a size that conveniently fits our plans and ambitions and tastes."[8] To avoid this there must be a place where we have arrived at death to ourselves – we won't get anywhere until we do.

"Absolute surrender was and is the only logical solution to finding our purpose in life in our walk with Christ"[9]

Romans 6: 9 – 11 says: *"knowing that Christ, having been raised from the dead, dies no more ... Likewise you also, reckon yourselves to be dead indeed to sin, but alive to God in Christ Jesus our Lord."* If we are continually fighting battles to die to sin then obviously our lives are dominated by fault and misdemeanour. How then do we cease being dominated by our sinful thoughts? Answer: - *"By reckoning ourselves alive to God in Christ Jesus!"* If we are reckoning ourselves as dead then we are declaring His death and resurrection and enjoying exulting in His new nature. If we are doing this we are confidently in the place of personal transformation

CHAPTER IV

TRUE PRAISE AND WORSHIP = RIGHTEOUSNESS

James W. Goll insists: *"God does not speak into the realms of mans possibilities, but God speaks into the realms that require His divine assistance to see the word come to pass."*[14]

Perhaps the assistance required in reaching the goals God has put before us, or the necessary healing we seek, include the straightening up of doctrines Goll and Wigglesworth speak of above, plus the removal of the blockages in us or others around us.

The root cause of failure is immaturity of our trust."[15]

To reach the level of spiritual development we now share in probably took many steps up the ladder of maturity. Some of them possibly required some reversal and re-establishment on the way. God may have other important steps ahead of us that our heavenly seeking will reveal in due time bringing forth what God wants. A place *"where God heals bodies and relationships, thinning the space between us and heaven.*[15] Experiencing the constant presence of God is the place we all want to be. Unfortunately, when we learn that experience in our Spirit some times our next step is emulating that experience in our soul by self effort. In other words: we so desperately want that experience we unknowingly begin trying to produce it thru' fleshly exertion in our soul. Realising this brings a problem. How can we ensure we are hearing God and not deluding ourselves?

Moses didn't have this problem. Miriam (his sister) and Aaron (his brother) spoke against him recorded in Numbers 12: 1 & 2. Moses godly character kept him in the correct attitude: *"Now the man Moses was a quietly humble man."*(Num. 12: 3 Msg). Our 'often self-hidden,' "I'm better than you," attitude toward others can kill the reality of God's voice. Miriam and Aaron found that out the hard way.

True humility puts us back in the place where God can do what he wants with us. It will ultimately produce true righteousness.

How can we produce this humility and righteousness when we are living a culture-directed life making us the chief critic of our society and ourselves?

The Bible (both Old and New Testaments) consistently urges us to praise God in all manner of things. If you are busy giving out praise for something it is hard to be critical about something or someone or even ourselves at the same time. 206 different verses in the scripture advocate such praise. In Hebrews 13: 15 we are told to *"continually offer the sacrifice of praise to God, that is, the fruit of our lips, giving thanks to His name."* It will cost us, that is, it should be a sacrifice to do this. It is especially so according to Hebrews 2:12 when we gather together to worship: *" IN THE MIDST OF THE ASSEMBLY I WILL SING PRAISE TO YOU."* When there is real sacrificial praise, with all of our hearts and all of our energy, it will draw the Holy Spirit and real worship will take place that can bring healing and wholeness to our selves and the congregation.

It is sad to see many 'old time Pentecostal people' familiar with true worship, waiting around for the Pastor or some more enthusiastic disciples to draw the Holy Spirit into real worship, then they themselves will 'enter in.' Praise is just as important as worship and therefore paying the sacrificial cost to get where God wants us cannot be underestimated.

It is also sad to see some Christians, victims of stoic Anglo-Saxon culture, not comfortable with demonstrative praise, sitting (or standing) back not really physically entering in, just nicely going thru' the motions, appreciating the lovely words and melody but without real abandoned praise thereby making it harder for the remainder of the congregation to draw on a directive, decisive, relationship with the Spirit of God.

The prophet Malachi anticipated Jesus when he prophesied that *"The Sun of Righteousness shall arise With healing in His wings;"* Any way we can get a full revelation of Jesus in our presence will release the healing in His wings. It seems strange that the word "sun" is used here instead of the word "son." there is no mistake. When the righteous sun (son) beams strongly upon us His luminary healing will flow to those in His shaft of light.

"Therefore it is of faith that it might be according to grace, so that the promise might be sure to all the seed,..." (Rom. 4: 16) Abraham *"did not waver at the*

promise of God through unbelief, but was strengthened in faith, giving glory to God,... being fully convinced that what He had promised He was also able to perform" And therefore *"IT WAS ACCOUNTED TO HIM FOR RIGHTEOUSNESS."* (Rom. 4: 20 - 22)

King David knew about this. He wrote:

"My heart explodes with praise to you!
Now and forever my heart bows in worship to you.
my King and my God!
Everyday I will lift up my praise to your name
with praises that will last throughout eternity.
Lord you are great and worthy of the highest praise!
For there is no end to the discovery
Of the greatness that surrounds you.
Generation after generation will declare more of your greatness
And declare more of your glory.
Your magnificent splendour and the miracles of your majesty
are my constant meditation.
Your awe-inspiring acts of power have everyone talking!
I'm telling people everywhere about your excellent greatness!
Our hearts bubble over as we celebrate the fame Of your
marvellous beauty,
bringing bliss to our hearts........"(Psalm 145:1 – 7 TPT.)

CHAPTER V

GETTING OUT OF GOD'S WAY AND LETTING HIM DO IT!

One of our biggest problems in the Church world is the focus we have on our own personal need. Many people come to Christ because of a need in their life. They may have received true conversion following genuine repentance, obvious authentic faith in Jesus Christ with bona fide expressions of His love and the veracity of the Holy Spirit. Nevertheless there are often still seemingly unresolved needs within. Previously recognised or even formally un-recognised needs are now stirring. The fact that we are still focused on ourselves rather than on what God wants is our biggest, sometimes unrealised, predicament.

How do we rid ourselves of these often unknown and unrealised situations?

In John *12:23 - 25* "Jesus answered them, saying, *"The hour has come that the Son of Man should be glorified. 24 Most assuredly, I say to you, unless a grain of wheat falls into the ground and dies, it remains alone; but if it dies, it produces much grain [fruit – KJV]. 25 He who loves his life will lose it and he who hates his life in this world will keep it for eternal life."*

Our prime purpose of seeing Jesus glorified is often sublimated to our being healed or otherwise blessed (which may happen almost imperceptibly in the process of His glorification).

It is the same when people are initially saved. The very familiar evangelistic text, Romans 3:23, says "*for all have sinned and fall short of the glory of God.*" Unstated personal need of salvation instead of ultimate glorification of God becomes the usual use of this verse. The realised sovereignty of our wonderful Father, altho' readily admitted, is often lost in the urgency of solving our immediate problem. The Apostle Paul was once heard to announce to the Corinthians: "*I affirm, by the boasting in you which I have in Christ Jesus our Lord, **I die daily.**"* (1 Cor.15: 31)

He goes on to say in verse 36 (Amp): *Every time you plant seed, you sow something that does not come to life [germinating, springing up, and growing]* **unless it dies first.**

This self-denial came second, or even later, to the realised will of God for the life of the Apostle. Often, when we are so engrossed in fulfilling our personal calling, we find the pressing physical and other needs disappear in our spiritual absorption.

The unwillingness of some people to die to themselves first, often means a serious halt to spiritual maturity and quality of spiritual life. At this stage we often regress into our regular, secular educationally motivated existence to contest God and other Christians with our version of how we think things should function – repeatedly a source of much anxiety and sometimes aggression.

We need to get our selfish selves out of the way so that the life of Jesus germinating within us will spring up and everyone will see the glory of God. Col 3:3, 4 - *For you died, and your life is hidden with Christ in God. 4 When Christ who is our life appears, then you also will appear with Him in glory.* (not always waiting to physically leave earth to do it).

Sometimes, when we are in a position of insoluble need we busily look for someone else, maybe some noted international preacher, to help us out when all the time we should have been refining the gracious presence of the Holy Spirit; looking to play our part in developing the culture of the Church we are a part of. This can put us in the place where the glorification of Jesus washes over all of us. Personal and corporate wholeness is a result.

"You gotta heal me Jesus" can be the worst prayer we can pray. All we have done is gotten in the way of whatever God wants to do. The *germination, springing up and growing* is yet to be completed so that Christ who is our life is not yet fully appearing.

If you are a consistent reader of scripture and Christian literature you will come across 1 Corinthians 13 often. Inevitably you will be struck by the fact that there is way more love available from the Holy Spirit of God that you have yet to experience. Cessationists (those adamant that all spiritual gifts died out with the last of the original 12 apostles) often glibly use this passage to refute those using the present reality of the chapters on either side (Ch.'s 12 & 14 – how can you possibly do this by missing the one in between)

One problem many of us have, who acknowledge the charismatic giftings, is to limit the outpouring of God's healing grace to the one gift – "healing the sick." (1Cor 12: 9). Much of the healing recorded in the Bible was a result of an unswerving spiritual life of the one(s) doing the praying and maybe the one being healed.

Even the utterance of the vocal gifts (tongues, interpretation, prophecy, plus words of knowledge and wisdom) can induce changes in spiritual condition within a listener. Particularly prophecy; working in conjunction with prayer and intercession, instilling changes in attitude and life bringing forth physical, psychological and spiritual healing, immediately and/or in an appropriate subsequent time frame. The prophetic is gaining prominence in modern Christian experience. Unfortunately the Biblical problem of false prophecy (Acts 8: 9-24; 2 John 7) is still with us. This means prophecy thru' a 'Prophetic Company'[12] is a surer form of spiritual encouragement and enlightenment. In fact this is encouraged by James, the Lord's half-brother, in the book that bears his name, **James 5:14, 15.** *"Is anyone among you sick? Let him call for the elders of the church,* [a prophetic company] *and let them pray over him, anointing him with oil in the name of the*

Lord. **15** *And the prayer of faith will save the sick, and the Lord will raise him up."*

Having participated in this form of actual healing there are several salient points:

First: the responsibility is on the one needing healing to call for the Elders not just to respond to continued teaching and prompting within the Church (The call then being the faith of the teachers). It means the rejoinder must be initially coming from the person themselves; otherwise there is no real unity of faith agreement from the person being prayed for with those doing the praying.

Second: it is the Elders who should be called. They must really be people of real tried and tested faith not just a group of the most popular people in the Church community elected by some unscriptural popular vote.

Third: there is no "magic" in the oil. It is the prayer of faith that brings the healing (v..15). Oil is merely the point of reference for the operation of faith and the anointing of the Holy Spirit. It can also be a point of reference for any associated repentance and/ or forgiveness for problems with other people that might be in the way of wholeness (Matt. 18: 21 – 35).

The 'impending – king' Saul, found the healing virtue of prophecy in the Old Testament (1 Samuel 10: 9 – 11). God gave him *another heart* (v.9). He met up with the School of The Prophets (v.10) and instantly learned prophecy. How did this happen? The object of the prophetic group was to verbalise inspiration of the Holy Spirit. Samuel, the recognised prophet, had spoken of this in God's revelation (1 Samuel 10: 1 – 9). God gave Saul the ability to trust God for a miraculous experience of the prophetic which he would never forget until he began to let his mind take over and jealousy reigned instead.

When the reality of the Spirit is present all sorts of things can flow and from an enlightened heart and can include healing. Modern day prophetic companies testify to this. *"All those signs came to pass that day."* (v.9). It is the same Spirit we have now, meaning we can do whatever we can trust God for today. All this is well illustrated as Elijah & Elisha travelled together to a place beyond the Jordan River. What was to happen was well attested by the sons of the prophets (2 Kings 2: 5). This prophetic company (who had obviously caught their prophetic ability from their fathers) again acknowledged the operation of the Spirit of God, now in Elisha, as the waters of Jordan parted at his Godly command.

In listening to these stories we sometimes get caught in the mechanics of what is occurring. We can fail to understand that the loving nature of the Spirit is constant. It is not a special category of Spirit that is suddenly manifesting for King making, for prophetic funeral operation or, on other occasions of specific healing. God is consistently loving. This love ministers continually, all the time. Differences in operation, (Ie the anointing for this or that) is the result of God ministering His love thru' the spiritual personality and capability of the one(s) ministering. What can God's love do thru' this or that person? What can God's love do thru' you? Enjoying God's love should be an innate ministry for all of us – all of the time.

Sometimes the whole of the local church body will be praying, at the same time, for the healing and wholeness of a needy member. If all of those in the body are totally united in this prayer it should be the most effective means of spiritual ministry available. Unfortunately this is seldom the case. There are so many differing views in a large body on how this healing should take place that the real corporate unity needed is lost. To overcome this problem it is necessary for the group leader to undertake the prayer and request the congregation to join him. This means he becomes the small end of a funnel. The large end now drawing in the attitudes and spiritual values of the people at large, being synthesised together by the words and approach of the leader.

CHAPTER VI.

MINISTERING HEALING

*C*hurch history is a chequered chronicle of some outstanding individuals receiving healing from God for particular maladies at some particular time. In contravention, at 1151AD Peter Lombard identified James 5: 14 & 15 as *Unctio Extremas one* of the 7 sacraments of the Latin Church. Lombard was validating the Roman Catholic's epic theologian of all time, Thomas Aquinas, in *Summa Theologica* (1150AD). This was interpreted for the English church members as *Extreme Unction* and became a spiritual remedy availing for the ultimate disease of remission of sins. It unreasonably says "*it prepares man for glory immediately*" at the time of death[13] (confession of sins to the Parish Priest must have slipped-up somehow as did Purgatory). This poor interpretation of scripture has done more to reduce expectation of healing from the Holy Spirit than any other single element in all of theology. It tends to hang over most western cultures to one degree or another. It is exactly opposite to what the claimed biblical reference of James 5: 14, 15 actually intended (see Chapter V.)

The Protestant Dispensational, Cessation movement is just as bad. In true dogmatic form it un-biblically, says all miracles of healing died out with the death of the last of the original 12 apostles. For many pastoral ministers visiting people in hospital and praying for patients there it becomes a duty with no thought that the prayers will do anything much to heal the one being prayed for. The person being prayed for is only expected to appreciate the fact that the Pastor has come and is representing the good wishes of friends and members of their Church in their time of pain and need. Encouragement of a speedy medical recovery is the best that can be expected in most of these situations.

The story goes of one such pastor, now believing in healing, visiting an elderly, female, Church member in hospital. About to leave, he offered to pray for her. She responded negatively: *"Pastor, Our Church doesn't believe in healing, it's not the will of God."* The pastor went around to the other side of her bed, opened her bedside drawers and began taking all the medicinal bottles and pills out. The woman became alarmed and challenged him. *"Pastor, what are you doing? "* He responded: *"I'm just taking these away ma'am, I wouldn't want you to get out of the will of God now would I."*

The modern missionary movement has put pay to all of the above views. Go to any young Church in Africa, South America or Asia and these burgeoning congregations will demonstrate the continuous vital healing power of Jesus in the effervescent flow of the Holy Spirit. Visiting European ministries have had to retract their previous cessationist views.

The question now arises: It's not that healing does not happen in western churches, but it does not happen in the volume and excitement of the developing world church. Even western Pentecostal Churches, renowned early for their foundational healing and miracle cultures, are loosing their vitality, now appearing, at best, like ordinary old-line throngs. Older western cultures, often founded on developing Christian values, became the way they are by continual enlargement of superior mind doctrines

– hence many different denominations. The cultural standing of old line Churches, based solely on strong relationships are now being lost to secular clubs.

Why is it that healing is such a dynamic part of the growing Assemblies in the developing world?

First: they are not limited by mental theology! The reality of the terror and trauma of the crucifixion of Jesus is upon them. It's not a matter of arguing theology.

Second: the fullness of Father, Son and Holy Spirit are fully evident to them. They are not bothered by the niceties of which one of them is bringing about the healing. They are more concerned with allowing the Holy Spirit to honour Jesus in whatever way He wants particularly in any way it happened in the New Testament. They are trained to believe God the Father will do whatever it says in the New Testament.

Third: The political and cultural situations, in many of these countries, leads to some form of persecution. Therefore anyone becoming a Christian must have strong personal persuasion to remain in a Church body. To believe the Holy Spirit will bring healing and wholeness will often be the only form of medical treatment they can economically afford.

In the west the well published failings of the western church are gradually encroaching upon communities leading to a mistrust of Church oversight generally. The deteriorating image of one denomination reflects on all of them. The niceties of correct doctrine are lost amid the public fanfare of Church knocking in the worldwide press.

One form of overcoming the obvious Church decline is by modernising the Church customs. This is usually only window dressing. The hard decision that must be taken is about developing stronger Church roots.

When Jesus said *"Most assuredly, I say to you, he who believes in Me, the works that I do he will do also; and greater works than these he will do, because I go to My Father."* (John 14: 12) He didn't put riders on the statement saying this would only be for the immediate life of the original 12 Apostles (plus Paul). Just the transfer of Jesus words from the Apostles to the minds of Church leaders was not His intention. He was interested in a transfer of life – spirit to spirit.

There was no doubt about God's existence prior to the 20th century. Miracles & healing were not necessary to expound the authenticity of the Almighty. Intellectual veracity was all that was necessary and legalistic arguments between different denominations was the vogue. Those who had no inclination toward involvement in the Church at least had little argument against it and ecclesiastical social values generally pertained. Missionary efforts had sluggish success.

Charles Darwin inadvertently finished all that. Now, with indiscriminate, often pseudo-scientific and media "support," western secular, anti God, intellectual society is well established. The western Church now finds itself on a downward authority and popularity slide.

However, the burgeoning modern missionary endeavours are proving the reality of Jesus' john 14 statements. Miracles & healing have become the norm of the rapidly increasing churches in the developing countries. It is now beginning to overflow into the western world.

Unfortunately there are very many ways of going about this healing! John G. Lake, *"one of the most powerful healing evangelists of the twentieth century"* was heard to utter in a sermon.*"Quit your meanness, you quit fooling with the doctor and the devil, you quit your secret habits and come to Me, and I will deliver you. That's the only road to God, That is the way in God."* [14]

Another powerful healing evangelist, Katherine Kuhlman is quoted as saying: *"If you believe I think it is a sin to go to a doctor to take medicine, to have surgery when needed – you do me a great injustice!, To be sure I believe God has the power to heal instantly without the material tools of scientific medicine; but I also believe that God gave us our brains to use! He gave us intelligence – He gave us will—and He expects us to use good old-fashioned common sense."* [15]

These views represent two extremes of healing – do we trust medical science for healing or don't we? We must get outside this argument if we are expecting God to do anything? It is putting everything back in the mental realm.

Trying to trim down the above into a usable state and find *'a key to answered prayer'* my journal recorded a quote from the "praye-master," Dick Eastman,*"To believe the impossible one must first see the invisible!"*This arose from his study of Israel's deliverance from the Syrian Army in Second Kings chapter six. Hebrews first chapter (Passion translation) ushers us into the most incredible assessment of the person of Jesus, His wonderful ministry and the awesome presence of almighty God.

Heb 1:1 *Throughout our history God has spoken to our ancestors by his prophets in many different ways. The revelation he gave them was only a fragment at a time, building one truth upon another.* **2** *But to us living in these last days, God now speaks to us openly in the language of a Son, the appointed Heir of everything, for through him God created the panorama of all things and all time.* **3** *The Son is the dazzling radiance of God's splendour, the exact expression of God's true nature— his mirror image! He holds the universe together and expands it by the mighty power of his spoken word. He accomplished for us the complete cleansing of sins, and then took his seat on the highest throne at the right hand of the majestic One.* **4** *He is infinitely greater than angels, for he inherited a rank and a Name far greater than theirs.* **5** *For God has never said to any angel what he said to Jesus: "You are my favored Son, today I have fathered you." And this: "I will be the Father to him, and he will be the Son to me."* **6** *And again, when he brought his firstborn Son into the world: "Let all my angels bow down before him and kiss him in worship."*

Our answer lies here

CHAPTER VII

PROPHETIC REVELATION

*T*o completely understand what has gone before may require a new framework of spiritual understanding.. It may even mean a complete re-education in ecclesiology.

Many times, particularly in leadership meetings, you will hear someone express an opinion about what has been said as "spiritual" or "not spiritual." According to your own values you will form a view of what was said and any succeeding comments that follow. Many denominations came into being because of something like this. Further examination of the contents of the discussion may reveal a political point of view. Nothing "spiritual "about that!

Obviously this can be a big problem for younger believers.

Following a re-dedication to Christ at Belmore, (N. S.W.) Church of Christ in 1964, I became involved in a small group Bible Study with several other young men. The group was quite disparate but all fitted together well in their desire to develop their Christian lives. Within the group was a young married man with an obviously bright, but poorly educated, background. In the process of chasing down meanings and directions of the scriptures being studied, this young man seemed to shine with Godly practical applications. This constantly frustrated my formative mental views of analyzing the texts before us. In retrospect I had to admit this young man always left me with an awesome sense of the presence of God thru' his utilization of scripture. This was far more important than my somewhat, less than "scientific" approach. He was not realizing the impact he was having in the spiritual realm. Even at that early shaping stage He was more interested in a vital relationship with Jesus than my nicety of language analysis. He automatically stirred the spirit which positively affected mind and emotions. In retrospect, even in that embryonic situation, he could now be said to have been operating in 'prophetically given revelation.'

When the acknowledged prophet Hosea spoke in chapter 4, of his book, verse 16, said: *"My people are destroyed for lack of knowledge"* he wasn't only talking about the current operating facts. He was referring to the reality of perpetual Godly life rendered in the Jewish scriptures. The ageless divine instruction continually proved accurate at any point in Israel's history. If they followed the revelation already given them thru' the prophets they prospered. But, when they forgot about this, which seemed to be often, destruction speedily came upon them. Spiritual principles never change. With the lack of godly obedience and the world wide increase in violence it is already obvious -- destruction is imminent.

When Jesus first identified His disciples (Matt. 10: 1 – 4) he straight away sent them out: (Matt . 10: 5 – 8).

Proverbs 29: 18 amplifies this when it says: *"Where there is no revelation, the people cast off restraint"*; Bill Johnson gives a more complete translation: *"Without prophetic revelation the people go unrestrained, walking in circles, having no certain destiny."*

All this is very serious:

NO PROPHETIC REVELATION = DESTRUCTION!!! --> EVEN NOW!

From this comes two questions:

1. What is Prophetic Revelation? And
2. How do we get it?

The New Testament book of Ephesians, chapter one verse seventeen supplies an answer to both:" ... *that the God of our Lord Jesus Christ, the Father of glory, may give to you the spirit of wisdom and revelation in the knowledge of Him,"*

1. Prophetic Revelation = the spirit of wisdom & revelation in the knowledge of Jesus.
2. You get it from "the Father of Glory."

LEARN HOW TO TUNE IN!

1 Cor. 2: 12 - 14 Now we have received, not the spirit of the world, but the Spirit who is from God, that we might know the things that have been freely given to us by God. *13 These things we also speak, not in words which man's wisdom teaches but which the Holy Spirit teaches, comparing spiritual things with spiritual.14 But the natural man does not receive the things of the Spirit of God, for they are*

foolishness to him; nor can he know them, because they are spiritually discerned.

Right now there are radio waves traversing the place where you are. There are also Television signals, phone messages and probably many other forms of electronic signal coursing thru' the air around you.

WITHOUT A PROPER RECEIVER YOU WONT PICK UP ANY OF THEM!

The evangelical and Catholic doctrine of repentance of sin and salvation by faith in Jesus is accepted by most churches. It is usually stated that this equals being "born again" and therefore meaning they will ultimately end up in heaven.

Unfortunately there are many people in our society, holding these views that never go near a church, all claiming they will be going to heaven because they have confessed these things. Equally unfortunate are those in existing church denominations whose lives declare they are no different to those saying they believe but never darken the door of a church.

Jesus aim was to build His Church. *" I will build My church"* was His emphatic statement recorded in Matthew 16: 18.

In chapter 3 verse 5 of his Good News, the Apostle John quotes Jesus: *"Most assuredly, I say to you, unless one is born of water and the Spirit, he cannot enter the kingdom of God."* Before this can happen the first reason Jesus gives for being "born again" comes in verse 3: *"Most assuredly, I say to you, unless one is born again, he cannot <u>SEE</u> the kingdom of God."* (emphasis mine) This is a reasonable statement; 'Why would one want to get into something he can't see?' In this situation the spiritual element of the "seeing" was The Spirit of God – personified in the person making the statement – Messiah Jesus Himself!

Seeing the Kingdom and being involved in it are also addressed in John's Gospel chapter 2. Bear in mind when the Spirit of God inspired the Apostle to write this book he didn't inspire chapter and verse numbers. These were a very much later English additions to aid scholars and preachers. So, there was no break between chapters two and three. Chapter 2 verses 23 – 25 came directly with the born again teaching of chapter three.It therefore reads: -

23 *Now when He was in Jerusalem at the Passover, during the feast, many believed in His name when they saw the signs which He did. 24*

But <u>Jesus did not commit Himself to them</u>, because He knew all men, 25 and had no need that anyone should testify of man, for He knew what was in man. 1 There was a man of the Pharisees named Nicodemus, a ruler of the Jews. 2 This man came to Jesus by night and said to Him, "Rabbi, we know that You are a teacher come from God; for no one can do these signs that You do unless God is with him." 3 Jesus answered and said to him, "Most assuredly, I say to you, unless one is born again, he cannot <u>see</u> the kingdom of God."

Obviously, those "believers" of John 2: 23 were not "born again". Any repenting, confessing and believing was contiguous on who they were, what they did and their reputations. Jesus had not given Himself to them in spite of their so called "believing." He knew there was no real spiritual actuality in their hearts reaching out to Him. It was just their own selfish bemusement incapable of hearing a call from Him.

In the Book of the Revelation to Apostle John, chapter 3, Jesus castigates "believers" who only lived for themselves saying He was about to vomit them out of His mouth (verse 16). These well appointed "church "attender's" had obvious;y not received Jesus into their lives; their knowledge and belief did not cause them to be born again They were rebuked, told they were loved, should accept discipline, repent and become zealous. (Verse 19). At this point Jesus was prepared to give Himself to them (verse 20). He opened the door of His life and let them in.

Being "born again" means **opening our Spirit-man to direct revelation from God!**

God has revealed them to us through His Spirit. For the Spirit searches all things, yes, the deep things of God. 11 For what man knows the things of a man except the spirit of the man which is in him? Even so no one knows the things of God except the Spirit of God. 12 Now we have received, not the spirit of the world, but the Spirit who is from God, that we might know the things that have been freely given to us by God. (**1 Corinthians 2: 10 - 12**)

The Holy Spirit is a great search engine: -

Psalm 139: 17, 18 *How precious also are Your thoughts to me, O God! How great is the sum of them! 18 If I should count them, they would be more in number than the sand; When I awake, I am still with You.*

Jeremiah 29: 11: *For I know the thoughts that I think toward you, says the LORD, thoughts of peace and not of evil, to give you a future and a hope.*

God has had a long time thinking about you – He worked out what's best for you well before you were born. He has some great treasures for you – **If you are listening.**

REALIZING REVELATION

How does one know they are receiving direct revelation instead of second hand information gained from someone else, from personal scripture study or some other doctrinal source?

Prov. 14: 6b ... *knowledge is easy to him who understands.*

Firstly: There is **no strain** in resting into the Spirit of the loving Father.

Next: **Lamentations 3: 22, 23** *Through the LORD's mercies we are not consumed, Because His compassions fail not. 23 They are new every morning; Great is [His] faithfulness.*

Thirdly: **Freshness** (newness) is a sure sign of the presence of God.

How you went to sleep is how you will wake up [plus anything the Spirit of God said to you]. That's if your primary concern was resting into the Spirit of God when your head hit the pillow. I'm sure you don't have to worry about your usual sleeping position. You do not have to worry about anything at this point. Worry will kill anything God wants to say.

Next: **How you have built your discipleship support structure will help.** There is nothing wrong with allowing other people's trusted revelation to lead you to your own. Nor is there a problem with honestly allowing the scripture to lead you into fresh revelation. That's what Psalm 137: 17, 18 and Jeremiah 29: 11 were on about above. The pillars of the truth of the Gospel will hold you steady.

Obeying what we know attracts God's attention.

The Scripture talks about a lawyer who wanted to know about eternal life.

Luke 10: 25 – 28 *And behold, a certain lawyer stood up and tested Him, saying, "Teacher, what shall I do to inherit eternal life?" 26 He said to him, "What is written in the law? What is your reading of it?" 27 So he answered and said, "'YOU SHALL LOVE THE LORD YOUR GOD WITH ALL*

YOUR HEART, WITH ALL YOUR SOUL, WITH ALL YOUR STRENGTH, AND WITH ALL YOUR MIND,' and 'YOUR NEIGHBOR AS YOURSELF.'" *:28 And He said to him, "You have answered rightly; do this and you will live."*

He pressed Jesus for more but didn't get it???

Obedience is a signal to God – for Him to trust you more.

A tender heart draws the spirit of revelation.

Job 33: 15,16 *In a dream, in a vision of the night, When deep sleep falls upon men, While slumbering on their beds, 16 Then He opens the ears of men, And seals their instruction.*

Revelation is for everyone **not** just for the specially gifted!

It's the revelation we have that limits us; but it also can enlarge the area of faith we function in.

Deception shrinks my area of faith.

It usually takes anything from two to four years to train a denominational minister/pastor. But, in Jesus case, when he called them he set them to work straight away. He used the "With Him" principle to do this. **Matthew 10: 1 … when He had called His twelve disciples to** *Him, He gave them power over unclean* *spirits, to cast them out, and to heal all kinds of sickness and all kinds of diseases.*

1. He <u>called</u> them and trusted them.
2. He immediately <u>gave them</u> power.
    a. To cast out evil spirits.
    b. To heal all kinds of sickness & disease.

No two to four year course or more before they could do these things. **He gave them** immediate .revelation about how the kingdom of God functioned.

Revelation will broaden our basis to work in.

REVELATION HAS MYSTERY

Matt. 13: 10, 11 *And the disciples came and said to Him, "Why do You speak to them in parables?" 11 He answered and said to them, "Because it has been given to you to know the mysteries of the kingdom of heaven, but to them it has not been given.*

Are you a disciple or just 'a believer?'

According to the Bible, Revelation is a mystery. It **<u>can't</u>** be hunted down, trapped or searched out.

It must be revealed! – we don't unlock mysteries they are unlocked for us. They are unlocked and revealed to those who hunger for them. His parables were revealed to the disciples <u>not</u> to others.

Revelation requires an attitude of **<u>Rest</u>**. (see John 15)

Proverbs 25:2 *It is the glory of God to conceal a matter, But the glory of kings <u>is</u> to search out a matter.* You are … a royal priesthood … (1Peter 2: 9)

We cannot enter into revelation without the assistance of the Spirit of God.

1 Cor. 2: 6 - 8 *However, we speak wisdom among those who are mature, yet not the wisdom of this age, nor of the rulers of this age, who are coming to nothing. 7 But we speak the wisdom of God in a mystery, the hidden wisdom which God ordained before the ages for our glory, 8 which none of the rulers of this age knew; for had they known, they would not have crucified the Lord of glory.*

The "know all" and the "self pity" spirits that rule our culture do not give visitation from God – **Faith** does!

Mystery should leave us with more questions than answers!

Tenderness of heart brings revelation which unlocks the mysteries.

THE QUEST FOR REVELATION

We can't get it by snapping the fingers.

Jer 33:3 *'Call to Me, and I will answer you, and show you great and mighty things, which you do not know.'*

Mysterious things are not hidden **from us** but hidden **for us.**

"Call" means to 'cry out in a loud voice.' – It is a reckless pursuit.

* Casual prayer gets casual revelation."

Psa 42:7 *Deep calls unto deep*

Eph 3:20 *Now to Him who is able to do exceedingly abundantly above all that we ask or think, according to the power that works in us,*

1Cor. 2: 9 *"EYE HAS NOT SEEN, NOR EAR HEARD, NOR HAVE ENTERED INTO THE HEART OF MAN THE THINGS WHICH GOD HAS PREPARED FOR THOSE WHO LOVE HIM."*

When **Prayer** is the desperate cry of the heart of man it initiates the beginning of revelation...

It opens up knowledge of God and releases the power for life and Godliness. It can give **"God encounters"** shaping the world around us.

Amos 3:7 *Surely the Lord GOD does nothing, Unless He reveals His secret to His servants the prophets.*

We need the revelation of the Word and the Spirit to renew our minds and prove the heavenly will of God on earth. We need a spirit that is hungry for things we have not yet known. If we only carry on with the spiritual knowledge we have always known nothing prophetically happens.

The acceleration of revelation is beginning in our day. *God is presently wooing people into intimacy;* so they will know how he thinks and moves.

Jer 31:34 *No more shall every man teach his neighbor, and every man his brother, saying, 'Know the LORD,' for they all shall know Me, from the least of them to the greatest of them, says the LORD.*

CHAPTER VIII

THE ASSERTION OF GOD'S FEELINGS

1. *"He who forms mountains, And creates the wind, <u>Who declares to man</u> <u>what his</u> <u>thought is</u> ... The LORD God of hosts"* [Amos 4:16]

2. God can cause you to think His thoughts ...?

   a. But only if you are willing to do them.

   b. You can't change your mind if you don't like them.

3. **Eph 1:13 - 17 *In Him you ... trusted, after you heard the word of truth, the gospel of your salvation; in whom also, having <u>believed,</u> you were <u>sealed</u> with the Holy Spirit of promise, 14 who is the guarantee of our inheritance until the redemption of the purchased possession, to the praise of His glory. 15 Therefore I also, after I heard of your faith***

in the Lord Jesus and your love for all the saints, 16 do not cease to give thanks for you, making mention of you in my prayers: 17 that the God of our Lord Jesus Christ, the Father of glory, may give to you the spirit of wisdom and <u>revelation</u> in the knowledge of Him,

I. ONLY THE HEART CAN RECEIVE REVELATION!

1. It is our heart that recognizes the voice of God and sees His imprint on a situation.

2. Repentance is not about thinking again it's about turning our thinking away from mere logic and having the mind of Christ.

3. If our Spirit does not win the battle for primacy with the Soul then our faith will always be at the mercy of our logic.

4. A logical, analytical, mind will always talk us out of a supernatural experience.

5. We need great thinkers but never at the expense of childlike trust and creative imagination vital to being led by the Holy Spirit.

II. THE MIND RECEIVES INFORMATION.

1. The Holy Spirit comes to each believer to enable them to realise, receive and inherit every promise that the Father has set aside for them.

2. With revelation comes the wisdom to find the heart of God!

END NOTES

1. Graham Cooke "Approaching The Heart of Prophecy"(Brilliant Book House LLC, 865 Cotting Ln, Ste C Vacaville Calif 95688 USA)

2. William Reading

3. Bill Johnson "When Heaven Invades Earth" (Destiny Image Publishers Inc., P.O. Box 310 Shippensberg PA, 1727-0310) Pages 17, 38.

4. Ibid Cooke Page 98

5. David Cartledge "The Chester Hill Miracle."

6. Ibid

7. Quoted by Kathrine Ruonala , "Speak Life" © Kathrine Ruonala 2019 .

8. Bill Johnson "Dreaming With God" (Destiny Image Publishers, Shippensberg, Inc. PA) Page 127.

9. Albert Hibbert; Smith Wigglesworth: *The Secret off His Power*" (Harrison House, Inc., Tulsa OK, 1982)

10. See "Walking On The Inside" © Dr Colin Crago, (Tate Publishing & Enterprises LLC, 127 E, Trade Center Terrace | Mustang Oklahoma. 73064 USA. 2015)

11. Robert Henderson, "Operating In The Courts Of Heaven"(© Robert Henderson Ministries, USA, 2014) Page55.

12. Eugene H Peterson, "Introduction To Leviticus," (The Message Bible; © 2002. Navpress) Page79.

13. Bill Johnson "The Way Of Life" (Destiny Image Publishers Inc., P.O. Box 310 Shippensberg, PA 17257-0310) Page 106

14. James W Goll "Changing The Guard: The Convergence Of Prophecy And Evangelism" (Elijah List, 29.3.2019)

15. © Roy Godwin & Dave Roberts "The Grace Outpouring" Sleeve Notes (David C Cook, 4050 Lee Vance View, Colorado Springs, CO 80918, USA: 2008, Second Edition 2012.)

16. © Dan Mccollam 2016 (Sounds Of The Nations, 6391 Leisure Town Road, Vacaville CA 95687)

17. © Morton T Kelsey 1973 "Healing & Christianity" (Harper & Row, Publishers Inc., 10 East 53rd Street, New York, N.Y. 10022. 1976.)

18. Compiled by © Roberts Liardon 2009 "John G. Lake on Healing (Whitaker House, 1030 Hunt Valley Circle. New Kensington PA 15068) recording a sermon preached at Philadelphia, Pennslvania January 30, 1914.) Page 8.

19. "I Believe in Miracles" by Kathryn Kuhlman ©1962, 1990 by The Kathryn Kuhlman Foundation; Revised edition 1992 (Bridge Alachua Fl 3215 USA). Page 3.